THE SUCCESSFUL GAME
OF REAL ESTATE

THE SUCCESSFUL GAME

OF REAL ESTATE

the Transaction:

95% PSYCHOLOGY, 5% CONTRACTUAL

VANESSA ALLEN

Palmetto Publishing Group
Charleston, SC

The Successful Game of Real Estate
Copyright © 2018 by Vanessa Allen
All rights reserved

First Edition

Printed in the United States

ISBN-13: 978-1-64111-119-5
ISBN-10: 1-64111-119-4

I would like to dedicate this book to my two children, Ruchell Jerard, Enid Jonel' and my Grandson Ruchell Jordan aka "Biem" all with whom I love deeply and has made a profound effect and impression on my life. When looking at them I feel my spirit in each of them. Each one holds a part of my personality which I can see and feel clearly. They have made an indelible mark on my heart. My children will leave a mark on the world. I would like to thank my siblings. Every time I see and speak with them they give me strength to continue being who I am because of who they are. I would like to thank also my friend from childhood who introduced me to this game of real estate Madelyn Ragsdale Lucas, who knew my ability and encourage me. Another is a colleague who I grew up with in this game of real estate Katrana Luelleun, who was a mirror when I needed one. Last and not lease my parents Sadie Mae Allen and Henry Mosley Allen as I am a bi-product of their union.

Above all else, I thank and is grateful to my God Jehovah.

TABLE OF CONTENTS

Chapter 1

BECOMING A BROKER IS ABOUT HAVING THE RIGHT MINDSET

For those of you in the real estate profession who know me, the number is great out there among you. You know me to be curt and straight to the point and a no-nonsense person. Therefore, you know first off not to look for this book to be lengthy or wordy, but straight forward, direct and to the point. The same way I handle my real estate transactions.

I deeply believe in my heart that **GOD** the creator of all, gave us the ability to create by means of his spirit. Deeply embedded in each and every one of us is this ability. It is up to us to know how to tap into this spirit which lies deep within our souls. Just like a well. If none of you have experienced this, when you look down into a well, it is dark and you cannot see the bottom, but at times you can see the water shimmering from the light above, you know it's there. Your spirit in you can feel it. You can only get that water if you put forth effort. You must first get the bucket and lower into the well and when that bucket hit the water you will know it and at that time you will with your energy and effort gradually draw the water up. When it surfaces only then can you smell, taste and drink and quench your thirst. So, in reading my experience in this game of real estate, may you come to realize that it is a game of bumps and bruises, injuries and fumbles but not beyond coming back or recovering. Just like the game of football you always have another chance to make it happen differently.

I can fully equate my success in real estate to the game of football. You are a quarter back in every transaction. An agent deals with, a team of people in one transaction a minimum of 10 people in order to get the job done to its completion. Your client/customer(s) if a husband and wife, Loan officer, loan processor, underwriting department, listing agent/buyer's agent, the seller/buyer (s), appraiser (second appraiser) inspector, home owners association, repair contractor for homes needing repairs prior to or after the closing, attorney's pre-closer and the attorney. Today's market if you are dealing with a Short Sale or Foreclosure you are looking at four additional people. This does not include other outside sources giving advice to your clients clouding up the transaction. (Friends they are in personal relationship with, parents, boyfriends and/or girlfriends) Did I miss anyone?

People come into this business of becoming a real estate agent with the idea that it is an easy job. I cannot tell you how many times at the closing table you hear your clients/customers say "I am going to Real Estate School and get my license". (Just because they saw your one commission check) Not realizing the stress they took you through to get to the closing table. Some of your worst clients/customers make this statement. These are the ones who want half of your commission to make their deal work. The house that they are moving into and not you. (Get it) They are the ones who claim at the last minute that they do not have all of their closing cost and want you to surrender your commission to make the deal work. Thinking that you work so hard and you will do anything to make it close. Those games never worked on me! When they claim they do not have enough money, I get up from the closing table and head toward the exit door. The loan officer plays the same games not revealing the true closing cost needed at the table until the day of closing. I tell you, this business is a game of psychology. You can only be a success in this game if you formulate a strategy for each transaction. No transactions are the same. Similar to a football game, no two games are the same. Even if you deal with the same agent throughout your career each transaction will be different. When the Falcon play the Saints, it is a different game each time. If you work with a team of individuals the only members that is switched out on the team each time is the agent, buyer and sometimes the loan officer. Still you have to form a strategy not only to win, but to complete the game/transaction with ease.

Chapter 2

PRE-PLANNING AND PREPARATION

*Without it, "Will make or break you
during the initial transaction period"*

You must educate your client/customer and know their personality.

Who and what you are dealing with is the first line of defense. <u>Question, who are your customers/clients?</u>

Female or male. The reason I stated female first is because the female in most cases if it is a couple, is the one who will contact you first. If this is the case then most of the time she will be the one you will be in constant contact with all of the time and she will more than likely make the decisions down to selecting the house. The man in this case just wants to move in with no hassle. The man just wants a basement and garage for the car. The woman the majority of the time is in a better position to purchase a home because they are more mindful of their credit or caretakers of their credit.

When a man contacts you first and he is married then he is the one in charge most of the time thereby, you have to deal with him in a strictly business and manly way (strictly business). He will more than likely make the decisions. And in all cases, you must know who to direct questions to. This is very important in communication. You will have a couple in that the wife will have low self-esteem or is extremely jealous, and I do not care what excellent suggestions you make it will be no good in her eye sight. You will really have to deal with her with more than the usual respect. This is territorial protection she is running defense. You have to always realize what you are up against. Do not take it personal, "its business". I will discuss this later under the chapter "The Art of Communication".

HOW WELL YOU COMMUNICATE WILL DETERMINE HOW SMOOTH THE TRANSACTION WILL GO.

WHEN THERE ARE OUTSIDE SOURCES SUCH AS FAMILY AND FRIENDS WHO ARE NOT DIRECTLY

RELATED TO THE TRANSACTION. (And do not owned a home themselves, LOL) THEY CAN MAKE YOUR JOB VERY DIFFICULT.

Chapter 3

WHAT IS THEIR FINANCIAL SITUATION, WHAT DO THEY WANT

*"Knowing this will determine if they are workable
or if you want to deal with them"*

This is the first thing you should check out is their financial situation before moving a muscle. Their wants and their likes must be in line with their financial situation. Once it is determined that they can buy and how much they qualify for, then you can move a muscle and begin the process. At this time, you must use psychology to convince them what their money can buy. I use what I call the Show and Tell methods. I send them a variety of homes in their price range and above their price range (which really fit their description, champagne taste but beer budget). This will verify what you are informing them about the market and what it will yield in their price range. The majority of the buyers want to keep the "apartment rent rate" that they are paying. You must convince them that they are buying a home which is totally different from an apartment; thereby their monthly payment for home ownership may be a little higher than the rent rate that they are paying. The Buyer want the largest home on a basement, four plus bedrooms and three plus baths, separate living area and dining area and a family room on a large lot for the same amount they were paying for their previous rent. Oh, let's not forget four (4) sided brick. Sounds familiar. Once you get by this stage of the process and only pass this stage will you be able to effectively search and find a home for the Buyer. Another major thing is to determine the location of the subject property. It will be based on distant from work, school district, how close of a proximity to family and or friends. I had one man who wanted an area based on how many DUI was handed out by a county. Crazy but true, he liked drinking. Never let a Buyer have you looking all over the state of Georgia. Pin them down to an area of true interest. The sellers think their home is worth more than what its true value is. However, when they are looking for a home the Seller now Buyer want to low ball the homeowner. Sellers sometime pull all of the equity out of their home and now want to sell it and make a profit and want you to sacrifice your commission. How absurd!

Chapter 9

THE ART OF COMMUNICATION (THE ART OF PERSUASION)

"Having the ability to convey in words and ways of understanding what this industry has to offer them in terms of what they qualify for"

"All of us perform better and more willingly when we know why we're doing what we have been told or asked to do".

"It's not the situation, but whether we react (negative) or respond (positive) to the situation that's important".

"To respond is positive, to react is negative".

YOU HAVE ONLY ONE MINUTE TO ASSESS YOUR CLIENTS, WHETHER THROUGH A

PHONE CONVERSATION OR IN PERSON, IN ORDER TO DETERMINE HOW TO INITIALLY DEAL WITH THEM.

TONE OF VOICE AND BODY LANGUAGE HAVE A LOT TO DO WITH THE TRANSACTION. YOU CAN NOT USE THE SAME BODY LANGUAGE AND VOICE TONE WITH EVERYONE. YOU MUST, I REPEAT, YOU MUST SHOW CONFIDENCE. YOU MUST BE CONVINCING. When showing property to a Buyer, always keep a natural expression. You do not know whether or not the Buyer likes the home. Keep in mind you are looking for a home for the Buyer and not yourself. Your likes and taste will be different from the Buyer and you cannot force what you like on them. They will see this as "you are only trying to make a commission" or hurrying or forcing them to decide. I have shown nice homes in excellent condition to Buyers only for them to select one that I considered awful. I learned early in this business to allow your Buyer to make the decisions, because if not, before the transaction is over they will change their minds because it was not their choice but yours. Whatever your buyer decides to purchase, you must as a professional represent them well with full disclosure.

When you lose control of the situation you lose the deal. You must always stay in the driver's seat. When you feel yourself losing control and the buyer and the seller is telling you what to do, TAKE THE STEERING WHEEL BACK! From the first meeting with your clients/customer, establish the basis for communication. Text, email, phone calls or smoke signals this must be established upfront in order to avoid misunderstandings. This is one of the top complaints from the public to the real estate commission," no communication" from the agent. In your Brokerage Agreement under the stipulations section, you can spell out the means by which you will communicate with your client. There will be those who will string you alone and waste your time. It is funny that there are those who think that an agent's time is not as important as doctors and lawyers. Attorneys charge a retainer's fee and doctors charge if you miss an appointment. We are just happy to have a client even if they do not show up or string us along and waste our time. We need to be more forward about the seriousness of our business with our clients and customers.

Chapter 5

THE REAL ESTATE AGENT

"A piece of Work or Work you to Pieces"

You must have a knack for this business. The only thing a Broker does is put an edge on the Agents business. If in fact the agent is a dull knife, as it were, you may never be able to sharpen or edge them. You must be able to identify this early in your agents. Some may not have the desire, drive or mental ability to perform or adjust to your instructions. Believe it or not, I have known agents who resent you telling them how a situation should be handled. They can see clearly it is going off the rails and respond to you as if "you are telling me what to do?" or it is no big deal what they just did. Agents act as if you do not know what you are doing. They want the reprimand to be delivered in a nice way so they can feel as if their error wasn't a big deal. The issues in real estate can cause you to lose your license and receive a big fine or better yet find your company in a legal lawsuit. I have known agents to wreck one real estate company and move to the next, demonstrating destructive patterns. You must instruct with authority in order to be heard and understood. The following statement is true:

We can't solve problems by using the same kind of thinking we used when we created them." –A. Einstein

This is a true tip, if an agent in an interview ask you this question, "What can the company do for them" their way of thinking is backwards. They are not bringing nothing to the table and do not realize that they are an independent contractor. The advice I have for them is this "Change your way of thinking".

"Keep your thinking right and your business will be right." This business is truly a hustle. In order to make in this industry you have to work hard.

Understand the thinking of an agent; this is not farfetched because Brokers, you were once one.

Take responsibility for your business. Keeping in mind that you are an independent contractor and not an employee. In other words, you own a business and it is your responsibility to run it and make decisions. Now you are the one who are making the donuts, investing time and money in your business. This is what it takes to make money and maintain in this business. It is not like a secular job where you report to work sit at a desk and wait for the boss to give you your assignment for the day. You have to give yourself assignments each day. Follow a regular routine and be consistent with it daily.

I like using the illustration of the ice cream man and the ice cream truck. Remember back in the day every neighborhood had an ice cream man that visited their neighborhood every single day. You knew he was coming and about what time. Well I equate an agent to the ice cream man. The ice cream man had a truck and the majority of the time he was driving subsidiary under a company, for instance here in the south May-field ice cream company. He had a certain alert song that he would play so you would hear him coming. He had certain ice cream flavors he would sale. An agent work under the license of a broker (Mayfield as it were). The broker is responsible for the operation of the company and to make sure the agent is acting within the laws that governs the real estate industry. The agent is an independent contractor and not an employee of the broker. The agent is operating his or her business (ice cream truck) and is making decisions on how to advertise to their base (neighborhood). The services they are going to offer to the public (types of ice cream) The type of marketing (the song or bell they are going to ring to attract attention to their product). Once an agent targets a neighborhood or client/customer, the consistency and persistency to follow up and follow through (ice cream man visit the neighborhood on a regular basis). The community will get to know their sound and can expect a visit to the neighborhood and a follow up. That agent / ice cream man is synonymous to the community in which they frequent. Really, a broker is a coach. There are coaching companies and individuals who charge an enormous fee to call you on a certain day/time and wake you up just to tell you what you already know. The coach is not going to do your job for you. Their job is to instruct you and follow up to make sure you are doing it. They push you to do! Truth, if it is not in you, you will never get it. Self-determination is what you need and no one can give you that. It will already have to be in your DNA or you will have to develop it.

When you are in a transaction with another agent, whether the Agent is representing the Buyer or the Seller; when they make a statement such as "I am not dealing with this anymore or I am tired of dealing with my client/customer" you must step in to take control of the Agent. When you lose control as the Agent, then the deal is DEAD. According to the real estate law, you cannot speak with the co-op Agent's client, however you can get their permission to do so. Or you may have to reason with the co-op agent to get them back on tract. Do it in order to save the deal. To get to the closing table everyone must work and do their part. Everyone has a perspective role.

When you look at a movie you expect to see each individual in the movie playing his/her part. However, it is going to be times when the transaction will turn into one of those Tyler Perry movies when you will and must play all of the characters in order to get the deal to the table.

We have in this industry what I call the "Corporate Real Estate Agent" this is the culprit. What I mean by corporate real estate agent is this; due to company closings, people are looking to the field of real estate as a change in careers to make what they think is "easy money". What they do not realize is that they have entered into the area of self-employment, entrepreneurship an independent contractor where you write your own checks. They change careers but do not change their thinking. So, when the real estate transaction turns sour or one of the parties has driven it into the ditch, unlike corporate or a job you can use "white-out or the delete key" and it is gone or you think you can start all over again. Someone has to get into the tow truck in the middle of the night as it were "go into other parts of your mind and play all of the roles" and get this transaction out of the ditch and back on the road. There are going to be times and more than one, that one of the characters are going to appear to be dead or die "as it were". The breath of life cannot be breath into the individual, and that is when you know the transaction cannot be resuscitated. Believe me, handling a couple of these deals you will know when to hold them and when to fold (stop and move on).

Top producing agents want more time, hate drama and is extremely confident and focused.

Chapter 6

HANDLING YOUR AGENTS

(It is best to have a few agents who are serious and ethical about the business than an army of agents who has trifling and unethical ways)

There will be times when you are tried by your agents. The relationship you need with your agents should be delicately balanced, approachable yet maintaining that "I am in charge of this operation." There will be times when the agent will question how you are handling your business and yet will not uphold the advice they are given. For example, a Broker gave up her business and signed on to work with my company as an Associate Broker. The first thing she did was give me advice on how I should collect my operating fees. Yet she did not uphold her own advice she gave me. I withdrew her from the company because of non-payment of her operating fees and not communicating with the office upon request on several occasions. You learn how to listen and receive it as just advice. I do not care how large or small the business is, you will find agents who are dishonest and will try and will pull all sorts of wool over your eyes. Even though they are receiving 100% commission with a small transaction fee; they want the transaction fee also. They feel that you are receiving enough or that you do not deserve it (counting your money). Agents, who respect their business, respect all aspects of it. From respecting the company policy to respecting their clients/customer. There will be times when you will have to make an executive decision and release agents from your company. This is when your company reputation and the threat of losing your license are at state. Never hesitate on that decision when the fate of your company is in someone else's hand. You will lose your license and the agent will move on to the next Joe or Sally Broker and continue in their unethical ways. Always stick to your company policy and procedures and do not show favor to agents that go against what is written in company policy. They will ask you to do things that they know is not right just to try you. When you sidestep the company procedures, they will not take you seriously and will eventually disrespect your policies and you! Never hesitate in turning over your agents into the hands of the Real Estate Commission for investigation. You can find another agent but you cannot start over in this business of becoming a Broker and to go through the process of becoming a Broker again if ever permitted to do so. Do not compromise your company nor character. I find that agents try to get over on the broker by not paying their office/agent operating fees. Normally the company will have a policy on late fees such as any other bill you will have to pay for your household living expenses. Agents will skip paying this bill and try not to pay the late fee. If you permit this, agents will mount up fees and challenge the balance when it is time to pay. When the company take the fees owed out of their commission when they have a closing, the agent questioned the fees owed.

I find that to be hilarious. They want their money when it is due them however they feel like the company can wait. The larger companies will withdraw the agents from the system if they are late and reinstate them when they are paid to date. If you compromise operating fees once, they will take advantage of it again and again. Set the standard and stick to it. I always remind the Agent that if they do not pay for their gas or electrical bill they will be disconnected. The

Agent must respect their operating fees, they are just as important as their household living expenses, they cannot operate without them. They should not expect the company to carry their load of responsibility and keep them connected in business when they themselves are not taking this responsibility serious. The fee most of the time equate to or less than them getting their nails or hair done or a trip out to eat at a restaurant. An Agent told me one time, "as long as I owe you, you will always have money". This is an agent who expects to get most of her commission at closing and still owe the company and continue to owe the company. There is a saying "if there is no charge or if it is free then it is of no value". I said that to make a serious point. Our services are valuable. If you fail to charge an agent fees or try to help them with their fees, believe me they will not appreciate it. They will leave you and go with a larger company with large office fees and pay them without complaint. They think that it must be of value or a change will take place in their business because they are charged high fees by these company. Rentals are on the rise in our industry and the commission split is low on such transactions. This being the case, agents are leaving the business. These are agents who are not willing to work the business to their benefit. You can easily make $250+ - $1,500+ in less than an hour not leaving your home, representing tenants or landlords. Money in rentals! In this instance do not compromise your commission structure nor compromise agent operating fees. I learned to never couple/group two weak agents together to work as a team. Keep this in mind the weaker one of the two will affect the other. Association breeds assimilation. Whereas both will remain weak and convince the other that whatever they decide to do as projects will not work. The main reason is that they are not willing to give their efforts and time to produce results. A farmer never plants a seed and expect to pick fruit the next day or the next week. The field take cultivation and will produce over time, your business requires the same. New agents think that going with a bigger company will make them successful agents. Really what they are wanting is their hand held. "WRONG" only thing you are doing is promoting that company's name. Agents fail to realize that "desk cost" play a vital role in company's fees. The more attention the broker provides to their agents the more cost the company incur, thereby the cost is passed on to the agent in fees, commission splits and additional miscellaneous charges. With a smaller company you have the freedom of establishing your name with your real estate business. Regardless you still have to put forth effort, time and hard work to make it in this industry. The majority of people who come into this business came from a secular environment and is accustomed to being told what to do and how to do it for the company's best interest. The new agents fail to realize what the word independent contractor means. This means to promote yourself as your business. Remember the ice cream truck illustration. When people see your name, they see your business. With big companies' people see the business company's name first and you as an employee. I see agents going from one brokerage firm to another looking for what they do not know. Agents must realize that no one can do the work for them, they are not employees but self-employed business people. I always try to instill in agents that it is not the company they are with but your "Hustle". Large real estate companies are hustling trying to get agents for their business. Some large companies are using their agents to hustle agents for their company also. Using their agents to promote the company and not themselves. (Using the pyramid structure to entice agents) Lazy agents are looking for the secret ingredient outside of themselves. It is the inner drive of a person that creates the miracle.

Chapter 7

THE LOAN OFFICER

(Really Who Needs Them)

I have so much to say. I do not know where to start. Well……. It is hard to find a loan officer that is knowledgeable, truthful and with passion for his business. That sums it up! If you find one that is truthful, knowledgeable and have passions you better hang on to him or her because it is hard to find another one. There are those who appear and disappear in and out of this business. When they decide to re-appear, they call back on the hard-working agents who are steady in this industry and want their business again, only to disappear again. A word of advice is "STAY WITH WHO YOU KNOW TO BE A GOOD LOAN OF-FICE IN THIS BUSINESS". Loyalty in this industry is important in order to stay afloat. I have agents calling me all of the time asking me if they should give a new loan officer a try; or to give a loan officer who is begging for their business a shot with their deal, I say "*NO*"! Stay with who and what you know. I find that if in fact you recommend a loan officer to a client/customer and if anything goes wrong with the loan, the client/customer will blame you. It is a rule of thumb if in fact you recommend a loan officer, you must recommend at least three (3) and let the client/customer make the choice. If your client/customer insist on using their loan officer, emphasis to them the importance of using someone that has proven their salt in this business. Buyers have a habit going online to choose a lender/mortgage company based on general advertising only to find out in the process of getting qualified that the upfront advertising did not apply to them. Emphasize to them that if in fact they make a choice without your recommendation and have a problem with their loan officer then it is their problem and not yours. "The Monkey is on their back". Keep in mind when going online you are dealing with strangers with no face! People online show you what you want to see. They bait you and switch. If it is not a loan officer I know, I always have a strong serious conversation with the loan officer. I introduce myself as the agent working with client/customary the Buyer.

I further explain my expectations of him or her and explain to him/her how I work. I also express how I expect all parties involve to perform accordingly to get to the closing table. You must express to the loan officer that communication is the key to making this process less stressful and easy. I am up front at the beginning so it will not be any misunderstandings once we start the process. It is always best to communicate with the loan officer before writing a contract. The loan officer will set the foundation on how you need to structure the deal.

Chapter 8

BECOMING A BROKER
IS SERIOUS BUSINESS
(WHO HAS THE GUTS OR GAUL)

"You must have Courage"

*(Keep in mind! Large companies structure their firm in a way that the agents promote their firm and not themselves) *The design in the company Logo *Control advertising templets, *Fee structure and the target goal for the minimum number of agents and offer agents incentives to direct agents to the company, somewhat like a pyramid. "DESK COST".*

"When a company or an individual compromises one time, whether it's on price or principle, the next compromise is right around the corner". The day you decide to stop compromising that will be the day the agent with whom you showed favor will leave the company because they feel that you should be obligated to continue to show favor to them even at the detriment of the company.

This is serious. You are responsible for every one of your Agent's actions. If in fact you are not able to lead, I suggest you leave it alone. You must do the right thing at all times and ethics must be your headdress.

You also must be fair and do not show partiality. You must adhere to your company's Policy and Procedures with all agents. You must always keep your hand on your business and your agents. Make sure your agents follow all guidelines. Agents will get you into trouble and move on to the next Broker who will be happy just to get an agent. It is always a good idea to call the previous Broker and just have a chat concerning the new agent desiring to join your company. It may save you a headache in the future. I have horror stories of agents running to my company trying to escape the bounty hunter (real estate commission) for violations committed under a previous broker.

At the beginning of my career as a Broker, I was told that the best agents to work with were new agents coming into the business. I knew that to be true and found that to be the truth. Agents in the business for a period of time who were not really good agents, who had not yet mastered the game want to join a winning team. Numerous agents who have been in the business for a long time fail to realize that the zeal of becoming a good agent and a zealous agent must start at the beginning of their career. This love and fire for the business must develop at the beginning and keep burning throughout. Because if fire is there and it dies down you can always rekindle that fire. "Selling is essentially transference of feelings and energy." Agents in the business for a long period of time, are still looking for handouts especially those who have never done well in the business. Agents must realize that they are independent contractors and are driving their own "Ice cream Truck" as it were.

For those of you who can remember the neighborhood "Ice cream man" knew the day and time he was coming. You also knew the sound of the music he would play and knew the type of ice cream he had on his truck. This Ice cream man had his uniform, his truck and personality that attracted people. If he arrives early in the neighborhood before all of the others ice cream men, he was able to get the bulk of the business. The early bird catches the worm. The same is true with this business. Agents must be about their business at all times, alert and energetic to attract individuals who are interested in the services the agent is providing.

Small agencies can offer a personal touch to their business because the agents can contact the broker personally and talk about a problem and not be referred to an assigned office personnel to speak with. Brokers of large companies are sometimes not readily available to speak immediately to answer their agent's questions. Sometimes not ever meeting the broker before leaving the company.

THINGS YOU NEED TO KNOW AND DO IN STARTING YOUR FIRM

First determine what kind of Brokerage Firm you will be running. Will you specialize in one aspect of Real Estate or the entire scope of the business of Real Estate? That will determine the amount of capital you will need. Several companies fail to remain in the business because of not counting the cost. It is called Desk Cost. Establishing their business was based on not the interest of the agents but on the number of agents. Charging low or no operating fees in order to draw agents. With the various fee structures out there now, you wonder whether the broker got the answer correct on the real estate exam about desk cost. You have some agents paying little or nothing to operate their business and they still want to pay nothing for their operating fees and have a truly 100% commission with no split to the broker.

They are missing the point. Agents who are serious about their business will pay for services provided by the broker. Similarly when dealing with clients, if in fact you know the business and is convincing that you can render the service to help them in their endeavor to sell or buy a property, they will pay whatever price you charge in order to get results. Agents who do not want to put skin in the game will be the agents who will not bring anything to your company. For instance, if you have bills to pay, you go to work to make sure the bills are paid to keep the lights on as it were. Agents think that they do not have to invest anything in their business to be successful. Those are the agents who want you to feed them and not teach them how to fish and to feed themselves. They will blame you for not getting business (catching fish). Yes, blaming Broker! Teach agents to have a sense of responsibility to their business. I always use this example when I interview new agents. "I only hold the license to your Ice Cream Truck to make sure you are operating within the confinement of the law of selling your product. Giving you tips and instructions on how to work the business. You are responsible to put gas in it, play the tune to draw customers, selecting what type of ice cream you want to offer and keeping the maintenance on your vehicle up and running. I have known agents who do not have business cards. I have known agents not to even carry a business card, but real estate is their business. Agents with listings without signs in yard, showing houses without lock box keys. Go figure! The first step to becoming a Broker is to realize what are the agents' responsibilities. Your major responsibility is instructing them how to drive, to hold the vehicle in the road and not allow the agent/driver to run off into the ditch.

Chapter 10

YOU MUST HAVE PASSION FOR THE BUSINESS

PASSION AND COMMENTMENT FOR THE BUSINESS

"You must have Love from the start because you cannot develop the love once you have started"

"Selling is essentially transference of feelings and energy".

What an agent fails to realize is this, "this is not a 9 to 5 job". Agents leave the secular work place and get their license and report to work as it were. I have seen agents come into the office and sit, read the newspaper and play video games. The worst thing that I have seen is when they distract other agents who are productive and constantly ask them questions about their business but never acting on the advice received. Every day you can find that agent at the same desk day after day as if reporting to a corporate job and they wonder why they are not productive.

Agents who continue to stand in this business realize that this is the only thing that they want to do and love to do. Whether it is the freedom it affords, the money you make or just the love of helping people, those agents stay in the business. Agents who have passion find ways to continue standing in this business. With the changes in the Real Estate market, agents make changes in their business to stay productive (changing with the times). This business forces us to change the way we do business. We use to be in a market of predominately representing sellers and buyers in the basic selling or buying a home. Now we are in a market of rentals, lease purchases, short sales, bpo's and foreclosures. Going after a different kind of seller who is not attached emotionally to the property (Banks/Investors/Mortgage Companies). With difficult transactions an agent must show skill and patience in dealing with these transactions. Learn from all of your mistakes; believe me you are going to make a lot of them. Just do not repeat them. Brush yourself off and get up and try it again.

"We can't solve problems by using the same kind of thinking we used when we created them." -A. Einstein

ALWAYS DO THE RIGHT THING

"Or the Wrong thing will find you"

S how respect to all of your agents.

Never show favoritism, apply Policy & Procedures to all (never compromise policies).

If in fact your agents see you doing wrong, violating policy or the real estate laws they will in turn feel that they can do it also. If you show favor one time they expect it all of the time. Doing things on their own, thinking that you do not mind (because you allowed it before). This happen to me one time when I overstepped my policy concerning Earnest money held by the company only with the approval of the Broker. The agent wrote a contract and stated that VanAllenWhite Realty Group was holding $18,000.00 without my permission. She turned the contract in with a personal check from the Buyer in the amount of $18,000.00. A personal check is no guarantee that the Earnest Money is good. I reprimanded the agent for that and since the contract had been accepted I deposited the Earnest Money Check only to realize that the Buyer wanted to terminate the contract on a flute. Just so happen within their due diligence period they were able to do so by one day. I had to wait until the check cleared before I could refund the Buyer. The only reason the agent wanted the company to hold it, is just in case the deal died. On another occasion an agent turned in a contract without the Earnest Money Check. The executed contract stated that the check was attached. The buyer refused to continue with the contract and did not give the agent the check. The agent had to pay $3,000 out of his pocket to the seller because the buyer defaulted and the agent did not follow through on what was written in the contract. They think their Broker will just give it back to the Buyer. Brokers have to abide by the rules and regulations of the commission in dispensing Earnest Money. That was a close call, because if the Buyer cancelled the check and the due diligence period pass, then the company would have to pay the $18,000.00 to the Seller. Again, the agent accepted the $18,000.00 earnest money from the same Buyer and when I reviewed the contract and realized that the contract stated that VanAllenWhite Realty was holding the Earnest Money and I was not holding anything, I immediately call the agent and reprimanded her and ask her who gave her permission to hold Earnest Money and she said "you did it before". *That's when I realized, never again!* My policy stated that only with "Broker's permission and no personal checks". Because I allowed it the time before she assumed that I will do it again. Remember I reprimanded her before for those actions and she repeated it. This could have cost the company an $18,000.00 loss. The agent did not have $18,000.00 out of pocket to pay. I instructed her to amend the contact and have the listing Broker hold the Earnest Money. The moral of the story is this 'NEVER MAKE AND EXCEPTION AND SHOW PARTIALITY TO ANY AGENT". Brokers must exemplify true leadership in order to get respect from their agents. Do not compromise your company's policy and procedures. When you do favors for your agents they will always expect them and in the long run, will show you disrespect and no gratitude. It has happened to me on a number of occasions. I know for a fact, if something is given free, the receiver believes it to be of no value. They will leave you go to another Broker who will take all of their commission, pay a franchise fee and a high operational fee and be happy with that. I call that indentured servitude. You will never be able to get to the next financial level with your business.

Chapter 12

BE A SOLUTION AND NOT A PROBLEM TO THE SITUATION

If a problem arises between agents of different firms, Brokers should always contact the co-broker and not the co-broker's agent directly. Brokers from another firm should not reprimand an agent from another firm. Always keep in mind that Brokers are responsible for the actions of their agents. Always advise agents that when a problem arise especially with another agent to contact the Broker immediately. Your agents must understand that just because they are with your firm do not mean that you will always and readily take their side in the matter. Never ever try to cover up a wrong doing. Sooner or later it will rear its ugly head.

There will be times when the agents of the same firm will have problems with each other. Brokers should never take sides. Always apply policy and procedures which is the company's "bible". That is why the Real Estate Commission require policy and procedures to be in place when opening a firm.

Chapter 13

POINTS TO CONSIDER WHEN START-ING A BROKERAGE FIRM

In deciding whether to start a brokerage firm, a licensee faces several important issues beyond obtaining licenses from the Commission. The important issues for consideration and resulting action include:

- obtaining a business license from the local government;
- selecting a market area and a specific location for the office in that market area;
- securing telephone services and furnishings for the office;
- obtaining proper insurance for the business including an errors and omissions policy;

- developing a bookkeeping system suited to the firm's needs, IRS requirements, and the Commission's trust account regulations;
- obtaining a tax identification number from the IRS;
- obtaining forms for reporting income and withholding and F.I.C.A. taxes to the IRS and worker's compensation for covered employees to the State Labor Department;
- developing a record-keeping system for contracts and other documents as required by the license law;
- developing or obtaining sales and listing contracts approved by an attorney;
- developing employment or independent contractor agreements for licensees affiliating with the firm;
- planning the nature and scope of the business for specializing in residential sales, property management, commercial sales, or a combination of these markets;
- deciding whether to organize the firm as a sole proprietorship, a partnership, a limited liability company, or a corporation;
- developing a plan for advertising the new

company and specific properties listed for
sale of lease;

- developing a plan for the orderly recruiting
and training of agents for the firm;
- planning a marketing strategy for the service
area; and
- Developing an office agency policy as required by the Brokerage Relationships in
Real Estate Transactions Act.

Properly addressing these concerns often requires
the assistance of professionals such as attorneys, ac-
countants, and other licensees who operate existing
brokerage firms. Simply passing the broker's licensing
examination and paying the fee to license a firm is not
enough.

DO YOUR HOMEWORK

If you are an agent with capital to invest then it might be a great opportunity to start your firm. Few people are able to take advantage of that opportunity. Truly low capital required and low risk with high reward. (Based on the size of the operation you desire)

Whether broker or agent, you are your business. Recruiting, building your business and management.

The goal of this business would be a business that runs itself without you being involved in the day-to-day operation. It offers you the ability to do other things like creating other assets.

The right mindset to have in becoming a Broker or agent is that of an entrepreneur. (A person who organizes and operates a business or businesses, taking on greater than normal financial risk in order to do so). It has risk as well as incredible rewards.

The success of your business is all based on "desk cost". How much will it cost to stay in business is based on the fees you charge, the number of agents and how productive your agents are. Keep low overhead, no inventory cost.

Your best action is the best-planned because it always brings the best results.

Question you need to ask yourself is do I need a partner? Should I join a franchise? Should I join a franchise based on the name and reputation?

Must have a business plan and great office location if you are planning on a store front.

When preparation meet opportunity, make the move by taking your business to the next level.

ACKNOWLEDGEMENTS

I am grateful to be involved in a profession that I enjoy. I find it rewarding when I can assist and navigate Buyers and Sellers in the home buying and selling process. When my fellow associates, agents and brokers contact me for advice I feel humble that they acknowledge and respect my knowledge and wisdom in this profession and know that I will assist them in whatever way I can to answer their questions or assist them in whatever dilemma they are facing.

I love and thank my children Ruchell, Enid and grandson Ruchell Jordan for their love and support in all of my endeavors.

I want to thank YOU, the readers of this publication. Finally, I want to thank the agents of VanAllenWhite Realty Group for the dedication and trust you have placed in me and my leadership to assist and guide you in this profession. Most importantly I want to thank with all of my heart Alexander Pate and

Catherine Henderson who was always available to give me the advice and support I needed to be a success in this business. However, the ultimate thanks go to my God Jehovah for keeping me and watching over me and blessing all of my endeavors. I am TRULY GRATEFUL.

ABOUT THE AUTHOR

Born in Atlanta, Georgia, Vanessa Allen (Vanessa Allen Howard) holds brokerage licenses in Alabama, South Carolina, and Georgia, and has remained active in Georgia real estate since 1997. She opened VanAllenWhite Real Estate Academy in 2007, and operates her own company, VanAllenWhite Realty Group. Licensed as a Real Estate Instructor in 2008. Vanessa has traveled throughout the country receiving certification in areas of real estate, and she is also a certified licensed mediator for the Supreme Court of Georgia. She has two adult children, Ruchell and Enid, and adores her grandson Ruchell Jordan White. She has a love for fishing and gardening, helping others and always seeks to make her surroundings peaceful.

Vanessa's Motto:
Revolutionizing Real Estate with Precision

Vanessaallenhoward@gmail.com
Vanallenwhiterealty.com